Someone I Love Died by Suicide

A story for child survivors and those who care for them

Doreen Cammarata
Illustrations by Michael Ives Volk & Leela Accetta

Someone I Love Died by Suicide:
A story for child survivors and those who care for them

Revised Edition - Copyright 2009 by Doreen Cammarata.
Original edition published in 2000 by Grief Guidance Inc.

Book layout by Paul Cammarata.
Printed by Limitless Press, LLC.
Distributed by Lightning Source, a subsidary of Ingram.

ISBN 978-0-9788681-9-2
Library of Congress Catalog Card Number 2009930323

This publication is designed to provide information in regard to the
subject matter covered. It is sold with the understanding that the
publisher is not engaged in rendering psychological services. If
expert assistance or counseling is needed, the services of a competent
professional should be sought.

To order more copies of this books please visit:
www.limitlesspress.com
or email: sales@limitlesspress.com
Quantity discounts available for non-profit and education organizations.

To learn more about Grief Guidance Inc., please visit:
www.griefguidance.com

DEDICATION

In loving memory of my mom, Barbara Vitale: in her life she touched so many people with her compassion and empathy; in her death she will continue to touch others through this book.

---She's forever in my heart and soul---

ACKNOWLEDGMENTS

Special thanks to my family for all the support they have given me: my husband and partner Michael for loving, assisting and encouraging me; my sons Christopher, Nicholas and Dominic for inspiring me with their beautiful eyes always full of hope and questions; my dad for his belief in my abilities to accomplish my goals; my aunts, stepmom, siblings and cousins for acting as a safety net in the depth of my grief; my in-laws for embracing me with warmth and support through these years.

Thanks to my friends and colleagues for your special gifts: Carole who gave me the insight and tools to choose the wisest paths for my journeys; my supervisors- Doug, Judy, Pam, and Regina- whose support allowed me the wings to fly; Barb who listened attentively and edited professionally; Linda who helped with the finishing touches; Jeri who equipped me with so many additional training techniques; Barbara Rubel who provided collegial consultations; Paul who put the final creation of this dream together. To my closest friends, a thank you for your patience and encouragement while I was working on this book. Finally, a thank you to those not specifically mentioned who nevertheless contributed to making my dream a reality.

Sometimes life doesn't seem to make any sense. Things don't seem fair. Someone you love died by suicide. You may hear people say "that person took his life" or "that person killed herself."

Many people who have completed suicide have suffered from depression. Sometimes we don't know when people are depressed because they don't always show symptoms, but it is a disease that can change the people we know and love into unfamiliar people. Some signs of depression are sadness, sleepiness, meanness, anger and loss of interest in activities.

Your loved one completed suicide. They were not aware of how much their action would hurt family and friends. Their depression which is an illness did not allow them to see any other way to stop the pain. Hurting you was not what your loved one intended to do, although that might be how you feel right now.

Feeling shocked, numb, confused, sad, angry, upset or guilty are all **normal** feelings. You may feel some, all or none of these. Guilt and anger tend to be the most common feelings when someone you love dies by suicide.

Wondering if you could have done something to prevent this suicide is normal. Nothing you said or did would have changed what happened. It is not your fault; talk to an adult you can trust about what you are feeling. You did not cause your special person to do this.

Trying to understand the answer to WHY this happened may send you searching for answers that may or may not be there. You might feel frustrated dealing with these emotions. You might begin to feel overwhelmed.

At times you may feel cheated… cheated out of your special person's time and presence. At times like this you might think of what could have been or what should be. You may be upset or angry with the person who died. It is okay to be angry and upset with your loved one. These are natural feelings.

These combined feelings are called grief. Grief is another way of explaining how someone feels after the loss of a loved one. It is a normal reaction to loss. With a suicide or unexpected death, your grief may feel especially intense and long-lasting.

People feel their grief in different ways. While you may feel times of anger, sadness, numbness or disbelief, you can also feel periods of happiness, playfulness, cheerfulness or relief. With grief there is no right or wrong way to feel. There are however healthy and unhealthy ways to express grief.

After someone dies, people get together to say good-bye to their special person. It is a time that relatives and friends show their love and respect to the remaining family members. Depending on your culture and religion, there will be a special ceremony to honor your loved one.

If you attend a wake or a viewing, your loved one may be lying in a casket. If the casket is open, it may look like your loved one is sleeping. It is important to know that this is not true. Being dead is much different than sleeping. When people are dead, they can no longer breathe and their bodies have stopped working.

At a memorial service you may not see the body of your loved one. This is an occasion to talk about your loved one's life and to pray.

You can speak to an adult about the final ceremony, the funeral. You can decide if you want to attend the funeral. It's a time when your special person's close friends and relatives pray and say good-bye to your loved one's body.

At all of these ceremonies, people will react in different ways. Some people will cry. Some people will tell funny or sad stories. Some people will pray. Some people will talk about other things. Some people may have no reaction at all.

Even if you do not attend any of these services, you can find ways to remember your loved one.

Remembering your loved one can be done a little each day or on special days such as birthdays and anniversaries. There are ways to continue to honor your loved one. Here are some suggestions:

- Say a special prayer
- Make a scrapbook or collage
- Write a poem or a story about your special person
- Have friends and family write or tell you about special times or memories
- Keep something that reminds you of your loved one in a special place
- Plant flowers or a memory tree
- Draw pictures of your special person
- Draw what you are feeling when you think of that person
- Visit the grave

Don't forget that everyone is different. What might help one person might not be right for you. Don't limit yourself to the above list. Find something that works for you!

Expressing your grief will have positive, long-term effects. By expressing your grief and finding ways to help you cope, you will survive this very sad time in your life.

Remember everyone grieves differently and what helps each individual will differ too! If one thing isn't bringing you some relief, try something else.

Talking with family and friends along with a trained professional can be helpful. Talking about the death of your special person might make you feel sad. If you feel like crying, it is okay. Crying with those you feel closest to may bring you some relief.

Being around family, friends and talking with a trained professional can give you a chance to share stories and memories of your loved one. Some of the stories might be funny. If you feel like laughing, it is okay.

You might have a special message that you wish to share with your loved one. You could write a letter or use a digital voice recorder to record this message to the person who died telling how you feel and include anything you wish you could have said. This can be done before the funeral and placed with the physical body in the casket or afterwards and placed at the memorial or cemetery. This may bring about moments of sadness but these will pass. You might find that sharing your moments of sadness with a counselor may make you feel better.

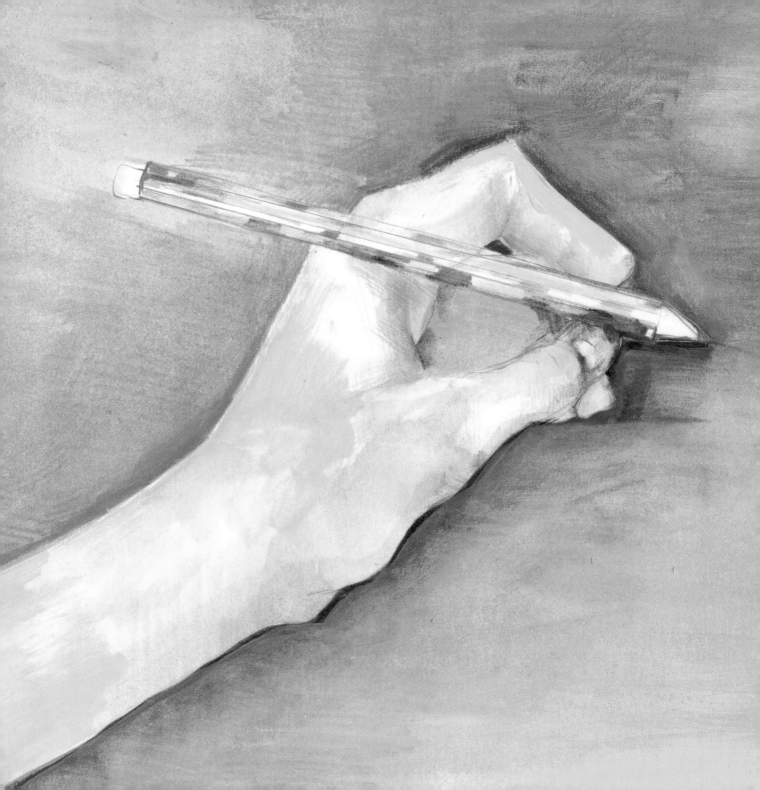

When you feel angry, try punching a pillow or throwing rocks into a lake. Avoid yelling at family and friends because this only brings about more problems and can make you feel worse. Let those closest to you know what you are feeling and thinking about. Don't forget they are also grieving so being open about your feelings and thoughts helps them too!

Drawing a picture or doing a craft like making a memory box can help you remember special times with your loved one. Use old magazines to find pictures and words that remind you of your special person. Glue the pictures onto a small box or place them inside the box. Include any items that remind you of that person. You can also write about your special memories. If you need help writing, ask a teacher or counselor to help.

Playing sports, and having fun is okay. Doing your favorite physical activity is always healthy. Whether it's a team sport like soccer or an individual sport like bike riding, playing is an important part of healing and should be included in your everyday life.

Celebrating the life of your special person can be hard and may bring about all types of feelings. A healthy release of these feelings offers a positive way of coping with the death of your special person.

Remember that everyone who has loved this person is also grieving. Sharing memories as well as sharing the pain in grieving will help everyone work through this sad time together.

About the Author

Doreen T. Cammarata, MS, Licensed Mental Health Counselor, currently counsels stroke victors and their families along with educating graduate students and professionals on grief counseling issues as an adjunct instructor at Florida Atlantic University & Hofstra University. As the President of the former Palm Beach ADEC Chapter (Association for Death Education and Counseling), she organized enrichment seminars and networking opportunities for her fellow colleagues for over a decade. Doreen has had eight years of university experience as an assistant instructor in addition to her full time work experiences as a school counselor for at-risk youth and as a grief and bereavement specialist working with adults and children at a local hospice program. During her work as a board member of the American Foundation for Suicide Prevention Florida Southeast, she served as a Panelist for the National Suicide Survivors Day Conference and was the recipient of the 2005 Outstanding Professional Award.

An equally important credential is that Doreen Cammarata is a suicide survivor. Doreen's mother suffered from depression. During Doreen's adolescence, her mother died by suicide. Consequently, Doreen understands personally as well as professionally the need to address this issue.

CPSIA information can be obtained at www.ICGtesting.com
Printed in the USA
BVIW12n0923121116
467672BV00003B/14

9 780978 868192